Pretty Punks

Also by Jessie McCarty:

Our Fairy Diary (I Read Stuff Bookstore, 2023)
The Bovine Huff (Track and Field Studios, 2021)

Pretty Punks:
Poems, Portrait & Play

Jessie McCarty

Magra Books

LOS ANGELES — BAGNONE

2025

Design by S. E. Pessin

LAMB PLAY was performed May – June 2024 at Facility Theater for the Rhino Festival in Chicago.

"Ballad of the Foxhunter" was published in *Sarka Spring* (2025).

Order from IngramSpark and www.magrabooks.com

S. E. Pessin & Paul Vangelisti, editors

magrabooks.com
magrabooks@gmail.com
PRINTED IN THE USA
ISBN 979-8-9926955-4-0

Contents

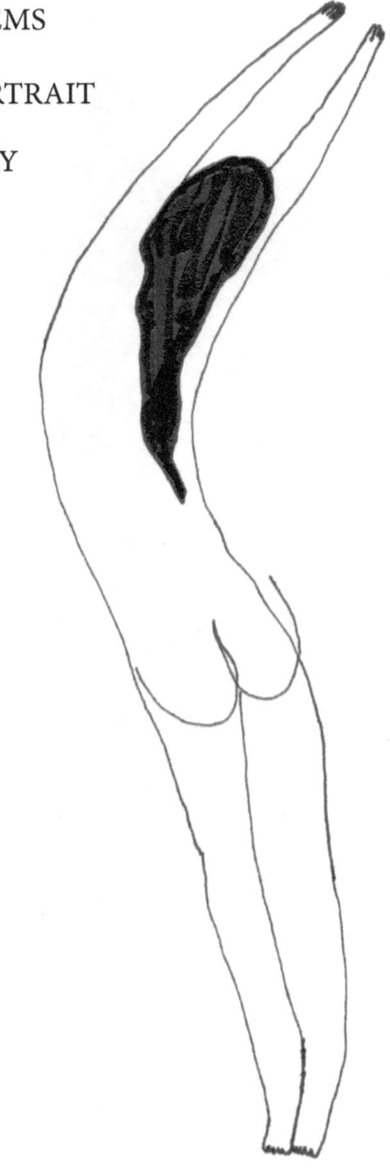

Pretty Punks: Poems, Portrait, & Play hyphenates the collected poems of William B. Yeats into a transmasculine cacophony of love and labor across the American South and Midwest. I have kept select original titles as referenced from *The Collected Poems of W.B. Yeats* (Scribner, 1989) and *The Poetry of W.B. Yeats* (Sirius, 2023). Select poems have been previously published in *Sarka*, *The Minnesota Review*, *Pity Milk Press*, and *Soft Systems Galleries*.

Pretty Punks is an ode to Irish poetics, my fellow Irish-Americans in the Deep South, and every trans-artist and activist living their truth in life and work. Le grá, beidh an bua againn. With love, we will win.

To be made a fool of by poetry is all any of us can hope for.

—Elizabeth Piasecki-Phelan
Forward to *LAMB PLAY* (2024).

Preface

To be Irish is to be political, to be aware of one's relationship to empire and the cruel realities of life as a colonial subject. W.B. Yeats, a protestant of partially English descent, had a complicated relationship with his Irishness, but strove to forge a new political identity for his island of birth with his explorations into poetry and folklore. His work reflected an acute interest in and awareness of the lives of his countrymen; the pastures they worked in, the pubs they danced in, the tales that comprised their mythology. Without romanticising them or hiding the unsavory aspects, he saw the potential for these scenes to become sights for national liberation. Resistance through persistence and existence.

The plays and poems collected here continue in that tradition, depicting life in a rapidly decaying empire, while gesturing towards something new. The war "rag[ing] through the sill" in the first poem, "Come Swish Around," is not fictional or metaphorical. These poems were written and performed as radical acts of community building against an empire waging war on multiple fronts, repealing trans rights domestically while funding a genocide abroad. "We dig and pray. / We dig and we pray. / Does it matter?" The *LAMB PLAY* expands on these themes, illuminating the violence underlying everyday work/life in the United States, how it "hurts to remember. And it can hurt to continue."

Like Yeats before them, Jessie's poems don't leave us with just despair. In characteristic Irish literary fashion, there's dry, dark humor. There are scenes of rehabilitation, therapy for the mind and body, a yoga mat brought to a folk show. Trans identity is depicted as a freedom, the ability to claim a life of royalty for yourself out of thin air. "Do I stunt? / No, king." More than anything, Jessie's poems are about the redemptive power of love and relationality. "It's us, together," they remind us, and that in and of itself is an occasion for gratitude.

—Colin Lavery, JANUARY 2025

Pretty Punks
for cheri

POEMS

Come Swish Around

My pretty punk,
& keep me dancing still
while war rages through the sill
of bed fire.
Pretty punk, move
against the night,
in your undergarment, lavished
with silks, soaked
in whiskey, with decorative
lace accents, worn for the boy
at home, waiting to be licked,
loved and memorialized.

Gratitude Hour

I am and I have it
          for every which way
something comes our way.
          I am, also even more so
we
          are so happy to see you.
It's us, together.
          I'm grateful at large,
and to laugh (so largely) so.
          Also,
for our lackluster couch, my bed springs.

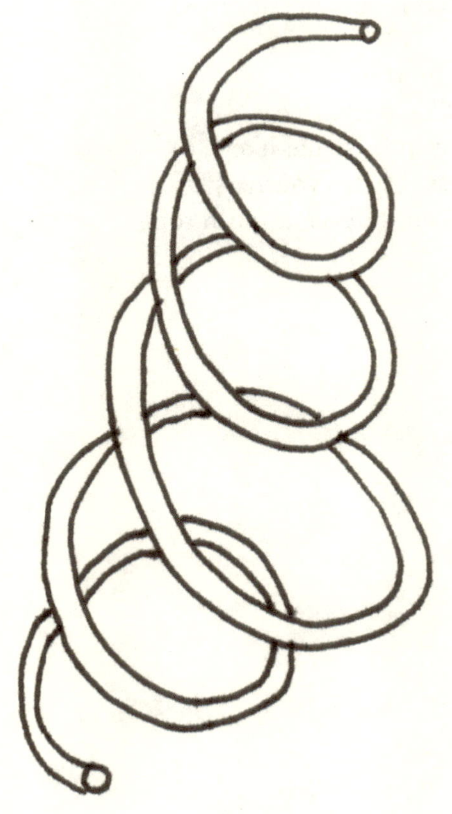

All I Have is Poetry

All waters are poems:
Routes of this' and thats.

I have wanted nothing
more than to coexist
in all of Red River's possibilities.

Grabbing mud beds,
language like a necklace,
interwoven in its snake-like
wantonness. My nervousness
slipped down in fever, a south song.

Queen Maeve

She goes to bed in everyone's bed,
transforms into a real bitch in her sleep.
On television, no one can live up to her proportions.
No one to watch her breathe,
No one to catch her fall.
No one to follow us both to that small place
in the fool's heart of beauty,
gone now from nights of straight bodies
kissing her body, my body
mixed with their bodies.
I go to bed, too
in hopes her body becomes something else to me.

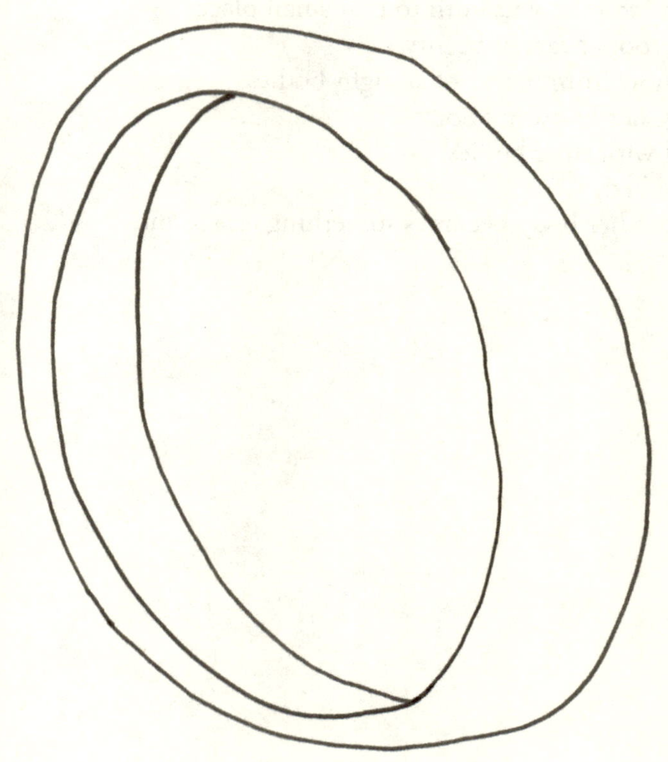

His Dream

To try or not to. He dreams
of his mother. By the bed
of malaise, do I awaken you?

He has such a beauty of death
on his lips. His face, bubbling
to the brim of grace. He,
who used to need me back.

Pink

Appears again, dream.

Pink as it was in proper hues
of orange-shaded indigo,
pink in my mouth sweeping
plate cracks with tongue,
pink as I bite on ceramic,
further fuel to my cavity ailments
and worn-down gums.
Pink is a direct result of rusting.
I'm gnawing on material like candy.

Two Kings

On Saturday, I pretend to be William B. Yeats.
Google, who were the greatest lovers of all time?

You as you love you. Me, as I love us, in a mouth,
crown of feathers, on this plane to New Orleans.

Gertrude Stein's poem *Cezanne*. Today is every day.
Shapes of my hands vanish, dissolving into glory.
I kiss you, I kiss you. My pigeon is you, all my own.

Our hands formed into another mouth.
Pleasure itself brings no weariness.

Being Trans-Southern at Rosella's Wine Bar

is fear me agut mo grah tu.

Man and I.
Do I stunt?
No, king.
Bad bangs.
Needle prick.
Impress him.
Embark him,
change him.
I'm different
now, not yet.

What Then?

Successor to love,
our married bodies
rotted cathedrals. You,
my little cutie, without arms.
Little cutie ending it. A little cutie
late for our resting. Baby,
I didn't love half as much as you.
The sinner is a sinner, too.

What is it with family?
Another boring legacy
stuck to my voice, going ghost,
scratched, weighed down by
granite slabs, looking like a prisoner.

Ephemera

The woods were around us both
and the yellow leaves
fallen like faint meteors
in the gloom past Benton Road
stood still, as it always does
on holiday, in ways so trivial.
My mother, once again,
abandoned herself in the front seat.

Her Anxiety

Onward, to the fluorescent-flooded archive.

I fast myself into some lesser
thing & my heart breaks.
Transit halts for passengers, but
never once does it stop for me.
I abandon library pastures
by starving for literary success.

The Pity of Love

A pity beyond all threatens the head that I love.

Does it matter if I considered a yoga mat for the folk show?
Does it matter whether those bodies inside such a grave were ours?
I'm filthy, this is what counts.
You meet me at the corner of California and Division.
Where do we go?
We walk, endlessly, nowhere.
We go out searching for shovels.
You linger, you're tired. You sit.
I graze down toward my hands (closed).
Should you be carried?
To carry you (under rocks)
built for you (working harder)
for you (without greed) is an act of remembering.
We reach the crux of location.
Dirt is my sound, every stretch is the soil
is a bow to your stage, love letter, midnight, changes.
You are still tired, I am still digging.
Kisses are left to unbury devotion

(where it matters) whether the music is playing or not.
The concert is over,
and the walk it takes from stage to bed is unjustly long.
The grass grows louder.
The sun sinks lower.
We dig and pray.
We dig and we pray.
Does it matter?
I just get your memory, and I just get to be there,
and I just get to live here, bent over and bowed.

FAGTHA INA N-AONAR

Therapist said, *You're going to want to need it.*
Treatments for hip pain included
floor stretches,
salt water rinses,
begging for forgiveness, silence.

My chest stays down
in a fetal pose with a furrowed chin.
My face stays down
on a scraped apartment floor.
My teeth stay down
chipping on surly, wood panels,
drool sliding across bedposts.
It is in these isolated moments
of help I ask him to love me
in all my inconveniences.

Spilt Milk

Every friendship has ruined me.
We have done what we thought
was an adequate performance
in leisure.
We have thought and done
more than thinking.
Soon we will ramble
into nothing,
thin out.

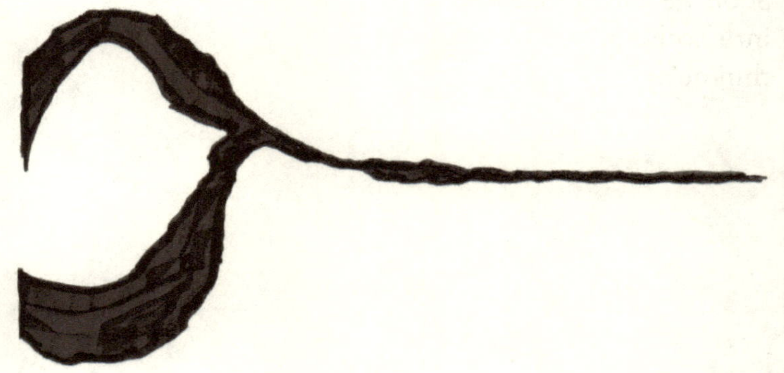

Self and Soul

On a run, it is the wind
hitting my face, collecting
smoke and thrifted bark,
making me warm with exhaustion and effort.

I met a friend on the trail.
It was you.
Over the years, I told you about my life,
smiling while I do it, laughing face forward.

The threat to our intellect was purple,
though I lied about it.
You had me set my head
on your shoulder, or I was
holding you in some way,
to talk and share notes of time,
of its passing or becoming.

So why should imaginations of men
long past their prime, remember things
that are emblematical?
Does it mean we were of
no use to each other?
Did it mean we could not

distinguish darkness from souls?

My self was the wandering risk
of girlhood, now a boy.
Everything we looked upon
was content until it wasn't.
My self was the final factor.
I delivered myself

from crime and shame and birth.
It hurts to remember.
And it hurts to continue.

Yeats' Coat

In which he made
by the mythology of
heel throat slog and soot,
wrapped up in song
where they sang it &
left its threads ragged and wet.
No one's going to wear it now,
he writes. For there's
more to prison than nakedness,
more to dying than dying lying down.
Plus, you've got to love the world,
as cold as it is.

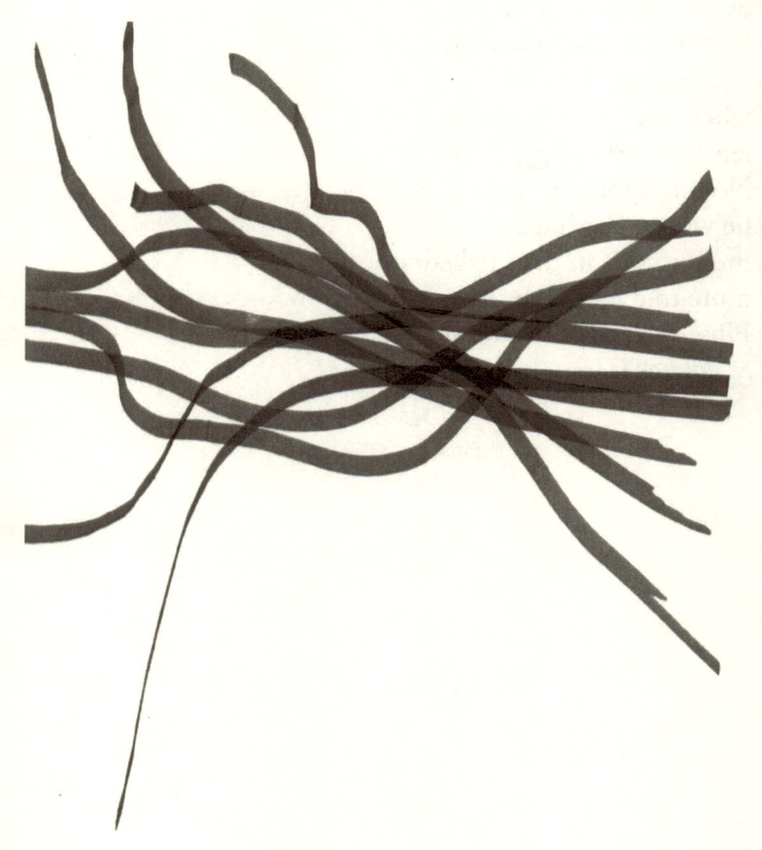

Ballad of the Foxhunter

Greed becomes my uniform, yes
but I lack the confidence
to wear it regularly.

What if his manhood
was my manhood?
I try us again
in the grass, in the mud,
wood, hut, and again in his house.
My brick, our room, stolen mirrors.
Lay me, carry me, bring me
the soft chair. Command me
to become more like you.

EILE GO DEO

Leit tu bhfuil fear,
mo grah go deo.
Caithfidh mé bheith imithe
ann ta uaigh, mar
bainise, no carraig.
caithfidh méa bheith imithe
ann ta uaigh.

Another Forever

Beside you is a man,
my love, forever.
Like a wedding, or a rock.
I must have gone there
is a grave.

My Lonely Goes

Is something the matter?
Is something wrong?

When *babai*
tells me *oh nothing*,
I have a sense
he is lying.

I was a cataloger for a long time.
I know about wrongful entry, I seek it.

My House

Correcting a place is a crisis in manners.
No catalog can tell me about misery,
daemonic rage, gambits, swingers,
of every wind blowing,
burials of pure devotion, good company,
how we imagined everything, or how
I hate work.

How They Wanted Isles in the Water

How I loved you, with you
I would go.
How I kneedled you
and refurbished you
like a barbed wire rusted,
like an ocean fitting into one bottle.

Like a shy one, with you
I would go.
Write more, kiss longer.

When men tell me I need more
texture, do they mean I lack
a certain appeal?

You want me when I haven't got
anything else.
You have me when I don't ask.
Reach higher, grope better.

You, shy one, coalescing,
lighting candles in a damp place.
You shy one, let it drown me.

To carry pearls in arow,
sowing mounds of sand,
for love.
And if it was a wave,
let it drown me.

PORTRAIT

He who works without grace is dead before the 10th year.

Here is the death of the Bull Rider according to this version: The Bull Rider, born one of seven sons, woke in the morning, like any other morning, with his brothers to tend the homestead. On the road to cattle, the Bull Rider saw something strange: a wild, beautiful light emitting off the farm, like the sun but far too cloudy to be, and sparkling, but much too close to be the stars. A white bull. He was dressed in a glorious saddle trickled in gold, bells, and diamonds.

"Where did you come from?" Asked the Bull Rider, who was alone.

"From the woods, far yonder." The White Bull gestured towards a deep, dark wood that led to the town's small creek, which flowed into an even greater river, which flowed into a gulf. That gulf ran into an ocean, a body of water Bull Rider had never seen, but wanted to. The Bull Rider looked around. A bubbling, small hope arose within him.

"Where is the rest of the herd?"

"As you found them," said White Bull. "Tending to their grass, as usual."

"And what am I to do with you?" Asked Bull Rider.

"You may ride me and take me as far as your eye can see."

The Bull Rider glanced back, his family moving like ants, too far off to now wave back. "And my brothers?"

"They will be here. As much, or as little, as you'll need them."

With this, the Bull Rider jumped onto the back of White Bull. From all angles, White Bull's milky coat shone iridescently. As his coat's radiance faded, Bull Rider found himself in perfect rodeo dress: a diamond-covered hat, white gloves with gilded thread. A pair of thick, new boots. He hit White Bull with smooth, silver stirrups. Together, they set off towards the creek, down the river, and so on, to that big arena of lights.

That night, they performed a series of immaculate rodeo successes Bull Rider had never known. His riding looked like a dance, rather than a fight. White Bull was his accomplice now, his co-worker. In awe, audiences watched and howled. Flowers and horns were thrown in praise, while children ran towards them for a picture.

It was the first time in his career Bull Rider won every rodeo in his parish. That weekend, he won the region. That summer, Bull Rider and White Bull won the whole state. At New Year's, Bull Rider was named the absolute Best Man in Bull Riding across the country. White Bull was named the Strongest: all 1,995 pounds of mythological muscle. This started a decade of decadence for Bull Rider. He vowed never to get off White Bull. He considered himself part angel. This white bovine is magic, and now, so was he.

For years, Bull Rider rode early and slept none. He declined chances for rest, for thanks, or visitation. He lived on cash prizes and romance. He lived on champagne and large plates of fruits, meats, and cake. Bull Rider even forgot what his family looked like and the farm he helped build. Though his family wrote letters, he never wrote. He'd ride and ride White Bull far off after the arenas and into the night. The moon would lead them all across river beds and seasides. White Bull, in turn, grew very tired. His muscles weakened. Still, each night he performed, happy to be working alongside Bull Rider in a field they both enjoyed.

During one rodeo, in their tenth year, White Bull was struck with the sudden need to sleep.
"Bull Rider, can we stop?" He asked. "I can feel my neck burning, my eyes running."Bull Rider looked down at White

Bull. The song of the audience muffled out all other noise.

"We can't stop!" He yelled. "I'd lose."

"We would lose." White Bull said. "But just this once. I am tired."

At 7 seconds, Bull Rider conceded. With his free hand, he yanked White Bull up by the ear. An accidental slap counts as an immediate disqualification. The Bull Rider had given up the contest. White Bull's magic waned. White Bull breathed a sigh of relief and flung Bull Rider off. As the Bull Rider flew into the air, so did his gloves, off of his fingers, and into the soil. Bull Rider's uniform formed a gradient of gold to a drizzly grey. His jacket's golden thread frayed, his hat de-jeweled. Bull Rider landed fast and hard in the center of the rodeo, right under White Bull, who finally collapsed, too, onto the body of Bull Rider.

Both exhaled short, pained sighs and died in unison. In mourning, every rodeo association assembled in long lines to drop off flowers, wheat, and milk. No one knew how to tell the family of the Bull Rider's fate, for none of kin had seen the Rider in so long.

Remember the fate of Bull Rider and White Bull. Their journey from this Earth was not pleasant. There has to be more to splendor than these monetary services.

PLAY

Introduction

Jessie McCarty and W. B. Yeats were born over 130 years apart, but their work bridges this chasm of time, connected by subtle threads, thin and invisible as spiderwebs but just as strong. The best art makes us feel like we have transcended some measure of distance, be it physical or temporal. As a "martyr to time," Jessie's poetry transposes modern spirits and objects onto the roadmap of the eternal, tracing interstates onto ancient footpaths, UX designers worn on the outside of poets, eternity on California and Division, deathless computer lambs on the Irish countryside. Tenderness and dislocation walk arm in arm.

Irish literature is redolent of the eerie, the liminal, and the unknowable; much of their poetry, both Jessie's and Yeats's, is cloaked in similar shrouds. A prominent theme is the twin, the not-quite-double, the reflection touched with shadow; Jessie uses this brilliantly in their poetry when they suggest that they are a double of Yeats himself, or rather, Yeats is them. In these brief, remarkable pieces of not-quite-prose-poems, Jessie interrogates the contradictions and sometimes morbid blackness of Yeats's personal life, grappling with how one can both love tenderly and hate obsessively. Seasoning this perspective of Yeats as queer double, Jessie infuses these poems with a queer lens, quoting Eileen Myles and Suzanne Scanlon. There is ambiguity, but there are also luminous and delightful pieces; take, for example, the image of Yeats using Google search.

LAMB PLAY is consciously operating in a tradition inaugurated by Yeats (and his collaborator Lady Gregory) with Cathleen Ni Houlihan, using the medium of drama and the stories of peasants encountering the mysterious and otherworldly, to political effect. While Yeats used these tales to promote an emerging national consciousness, Jessie's work is focused on interiority, examining the journey and psychology of an individual, their guilt, their frustration, and their anguish. *LAMB PLAY* also incorporates the liminality and encounter with the supernatural, blending the ancient and the absurd in a way that feels both traditional and ripe with freshness. Rather than a singular, nation-building encounter with a supernatural being, *LAMB PLAY* is but one glimpse in a quest, potentially of epic proportions, taking place in the liminal zone between life and death, ritual and betrayal.

I attended the final performance of *LAMB PLAY* on June 28, 2024, directed by Ryne Nardecchia. It was frightening to behold; the green LED glow from the scythe and the computer glitch-like sounds of the lamb's cough made it seem as close to science fiction as to Irish folklore. And the surprise, horror, and shock when the lamb's head is first lopped off: a deeply visceral drama to behold. It was also grimly funny; the third time the lamb was reanimated, a bit of spinal cord was still sticking out of the neck. The evil spirit wore kitten heels. The way it was directed had a hint of playfulness, and the audience laughed at the curse words. Nonetheless, I came away from the production feeling like I had witnessed something deeply sad. It was emblematic of futility, the thwarting of ritual, the desecration of the sacred. It created ripples throughout the play of guilt, ritual, and redemption. Combining elements of the ancient and the futuristic, in this way, Nardecchia's production of *LAMB PLAY* represented a collapse of spacetime.

To my surprise, the text of *LAMB PLAY* was even darker; the stage directions, lost on a live audience, include missives such as "the spirits of the dead are at last buried," the sky is described as "darker than usual, horror-ish, ominous, fated." The reaper is "tall, lingering, breathing, and eternal." That the spirit of death itself is specified as breathing seems magnificent and terrible, another visceral

layer on top of the visceral lasagna. That the grim reaper
gets bored, or tired, or overwhelmed with the horror, makes
them a sympathetic character on the page, while they were
simply fearsome in performance.

LAMB PLAY's timespan, too, feels unspooled on the
page, where it was compressed on the stage. There is new
grief and grimness, too; being unable to see the lamb
reanimated before our eyes makes the vivid blackness of
its repeated death stand out in darker contrast. There is
constant pain, death, grief, with the only reprieve being
the few pages between the dialogue, and they too bespeak
only the silence of night. Tonight, as the grim reaper says, is
every night.

This new collection of writing is something to pay
attention to. To listen to new voices and read new words is
to be reminded of what makes people human. Literature is
a way for us to be reborn constantly, beheld anew by those
who care for us. To be made a fool of by poetry is all any of
us can hope for.

—Elizabeth Piasecki-Phelan,
2024

LAMB PLAY

LAMB PLAY as performed on May – June 2024 at Facility Theater for the Rhino Festival in Chicago.

It was originally performed by Dana Pepowski as the Shepherd and Niky Crawford as the Grim Reaper.

Direction: Ryne Nardecchia.
Stage Management: Niky Crawford.
Set design: Dakota Brown.
Production: The Runaways Lab Theater.
Poster design: Lily Cozzens.
Prop design: Maya Muerhoff, Ash Barton, Rio Santos.
Costume design: Vei Kligman.
Audio and Video Design: Eric Breden
Set and Lighting: Dakota Brown

FIRST NIGHT

[*Setting: It is night, near a well.*]

[SHEPHERD *nestles a plush* LAMB *in their arms.*
SHEPHERD *drags a large bucket of water toward
something we cannot see.*]

GRIM REAPER

[*off stage*] Folklorically, it is a custom to throw away water,
to make an offer, to cry out, to struggle.

[SHEPHERD *drags themselves and a bucket upward,
worriedly determined, but unsure.* LAMB *coughs
faintly, then intensely.*]

SHEPHERD

[*to self.*] "Take care of the water;" or, from the Irish, "Away
with yourself from the water"

SHEPHERD

Ugh. But I haven't done anything wrong! I haven't done
anything wrong! What have I done wrong?

LAMB

[*coughs.*]

SHEPHERD

No, tell me. Tell me! What is it I have done wrong?

[LAMB *says nothing except more cough.* SHEPHERD
glances periodically to LAMB, *held like a child.*]

SHEPHERD

Please, LAMB. I will make this right. I will fix this. But we
have to reach this hill first.

[*It is still nighttime, now darker than usual, horror-
ish, ominous, fated.* LAMB *cries, sensing something
foreboding.*]

[*And a light comes streaming beneath from both of
their bower. The spirits of the dead are last buried.*]

[*Enter* GRIM REAPER, *they stand knowing in the dark
corner.*]

[SHEPHERD *arrives at their destination. A well atop
a very tall hill. Very night-night. Rested, yet withered,
the* SHEPHERD *pours the pail of water into and out of
the well. They set* LAMB *gently aside to watch.*]

SHEPHERD

See, LAMB? See how I carry this in, and out, and pour? Do
you see how hard we worked to get here?

LAMB

[*nods.*]

SHEPHERD

And do you see now how I will fix this? Do you how I will
fix this for us? How I will make everything better? "Take
care of the water;" "Away with yourself from the water"

Take care of the water. Away with yourself from the water.

[LAMB *sits, coughing and crying and aching in the
silence.*]

SHEPHERD

[*sighing quickly*] No, no, see? Away with the water! [*pours*]
Take care of the water [*pours*] See? Away! Take! [*pours*]
[*spills*], With the—

[*From the dark corner of the world, enter the edges of* GRIM REAPER. *Smoke emerges out of their cloak. They hold a scythe with a lamp attached. Tall, lingering, breathing, and eternal.*]

[SHEPHERD *drops the water in fear.*]

SHEPHERD

O! Cruel, Faithful spirit. Why have you come? Please. Your lack of speech is fearful to me.

[SHEPHERD *reaches for* LAMB, *protective.*]

GRIM REAPER

Ghost to the Mold, it is your child's time.

SHEPHERD

Please… I'll come crowning. I'll overcome this. I've been repenting, see? I'm giving back to the water. [*crying, crawling*] Let her live… please—

GRIM REAPER

No.

[GRIM REAPER *hovers their scythe high. A harsh screech is heard from* SHEPHERD. *A* LAMB *sacrifice.*]

[LAMB *lays down moaning by the Earth and dies.*]

[*The night is night, but quieter.*]

[*This continues every night, the same hour for three nights.* GRIM REAPER *returns.* LAMB *is ended, over and over, no exceptions.* GRIM REAPER, *wandering,* SHEPHERD, *in pain, away with the water. Our* LAMB *lays down, projected, falling endlessly, then moans, and dies.*]

NIGHT TWO

[SHEPHERD, LAMB, *and* GRIM REAPER *are standing near one another.*]

SHEPHERD

Why are you doing this?

GRIM REAPER

[*shrugs.*]

[GRIM REAPER *hovers their scythe high. A harsh screech is heard from* SHEPHERD. *A* LAMB *sacrifice. The night is still night, but quieter now.*]

NIGHT THREE

[SHEPHERD, LAMB, *and* GRIM REAPER *are standing near one another.*]

SHEPHERD

[*gasping, drenched, begging*] Please!!!! I cannot take any more sacrifice. Take my water, take my soul. I cannot bear to watch LAMB die again, and again, night after night. After night and night. And every night.

GRIM REAPER

But tonight is every night.

SHEPHERD

Please—

[GRIM REAPER *hovers their scythe high. A harsh screech is heard from* SHEPHERD. *A* LAMB *sacrifice.*]

[*The night is still night, but quieter now.*]

[*After this had happened three times,* GRIM REAPER

was sent for, meaning he was also tired, whether from the task or horror running its course. GRIM REAPER *gets bored. By the strength of this exorcism, the spirit of the dead* LAMB *is finally laid to rest. The recurring death of* LAMB *appears no more.*]

<u>LAST NIGHT</u>

[GRIM REAPER *hovers over* SHEPHERD, *over a makeshift tomb, created by* SHEPHERD, *from the well and with a silent hand of mourning, offers themselves a condolence.*]

GRIM REAPER
[*Hand to heart and hand to* LAMB *head*] Tonight, and then tomorrow. There may be something else for you to carry. More water, more sheep.

SHEPHERD
There is nothing left for me to love.

[GRIM REAPER *raises their finger as if to speak.*]

SHEPHERD
No. I have chosen the wrong career. I have chosen the wrong animal to raise. I have failed to raise myself. And I haven't even done anything wrong. I haven't done anything wrong! I haven't done anything!

[GRIM REAPER *shuffles awkwardly, waiting to interject their opinion no one has asked for.*]

SHEPHERD
And this is just so sad. Of course that would happen to me. Take care of the water, Pour!!! Away with yourself with the water!! Pour!! And I haven't even done anything wrong!!!!!!!!

[GRIM REAPER *exits.*]

[SHEPHERD *remains, alone.*]

SHEPHERD

Neither more found
nor in dried well water,
a lamb grave is finally laid to rest
by the Shephard's hands
made up of earth, water, clay.